DEDICATION

To my friends who share in the joys and the struggles
of parenthood. May this book give you wisdom and
courage.

Tommy McGregor

CONTENTS

Tommy McGregor

PREFACE

Regardless of how much you think you may know about social media and teenagers today, the truth is your knowledge and understanding will soon need updating. This is because the tech culture of our society is always changing, and it is doing so very rapidly. I know this because I have worked with teenagers for over 20 years. Since that time, we have walked from the origins of the Internet and flip phones with a new feature called texting, all the way to today where social networking is the king of the media jungle.

In this little book, I hope to help you understand more about the influence of social media on teenagers as well as educate you on my list of the top ten most popular social media platforms currently available. I will teach you how social media works as well as why it is so important to teenagers. I will clue you in to the dangers of those ten sites/apps, and give you guidelines for how to lead teenagers to be healthier and more responsible online.

This book is primarily for parents. I promise it will not self-destruct if you are not a parent, but I am primarily addressing parents because I feel that parents are the ones who need to know this information the most. As a parent myself, I know that need all too well. Secondarily, this book needs to be read by grandparents, uncles and aunts, school and church leaders, and anyone else who has a direct connection to a teenager or a pre-teen.

In the first chapter, I will lay out why I think social media connects so much to teenagers. As you will soon see, it is much more than just a novelty interest. The second chapter will help you learn more about social media and how it works. This will begin to pave the way for chapter three which will present ten popular social media platforms, how to use them, and what to look out for. In the last chapter of the book, I will give some guidelines and suggestions for how to lead your kids to be safe online.

This book is short for a reason. I could have lined page after page of examples and stories about dangers of teenagers and social media, but you have all heard enough stories. You need practical insight and advice to quickly turn around and put the content of this book into practice. I hope that this book will help you do that.

Tommy McGregor
@tommymcgregor (Twitter)

CHAPTER 1

GLASS HOUSES IN A SELFIE WORLD

"Social media has made the web all about me, me, me." *Erik Qualman, author of Socialnomics*

Do you remember the first time you ever got on the internet? For me, it was 1995, and I was in my second year of grad school when I heard that I could search for topical information on the computers in the lab. I didn't really understand at the time what the "web" actually was, but I was willing to give it a try. I recall typing in the word "football" in the search engine and being presented with a simple recorded history of the American version of the sport, filled with pictures of leather helmets and charts with broken records. I do not remember being overly impressed, but soon I would learn more about this new feature, as well as something called email, a great new site called "Yahoo," and that high pitched dial-up sound that can best be written as, "Pshhkkkrrrkakingkakingkak-ingtshchchcchchcch, ding, dang, ding."

Not once, though, during that time did I think that I was observing the beginning of a new era, much like someone might have while driving a motorized car in the early 20th century or making popcorn in a microwave, fifty years later. But, that is what was happening. Not long after that day, more websites began to develop and the world was ushered into the Information Age. From that point on, people knew that they could find out anything, or at least most things, on the internet.

Twenty years have passed since that first internet surf, and now the internet contains 644 million active websites ranging from pop culture and faith, to education, politics, and (still) a thorough definition of American football. Yet, with all of its positive and helpful features, the internet also hosts its share of dangerous content that can send an individual soaring to a place of distraction, disorder, and dysfunction.

Throughout this age of information, the Internet has allowed for many other inventions to become possible. Digital, mobile, and wireless technologies are three of the most significant advancements that have come about as the World Wide Web has moved into our lives and become a normal part of our daily lives. Today, we can barely remember life without these modern conveniences, yet we sometimes wonder if they have made us better or worse of a society as a whole.

21st Century Teenagers

Technology is not the only thing that has developed in the past couple of decades: I give you the 21st century American teenager. The world has helped this current teenage generation grow up to be an independent, well-informed, globally connected young person who is years ahead of his development and capacity for maturity. Today's society teaches teens that the world is their own, and that they are ready to handle it. More than ever before, culture defines identity, status, value, and success, and, of course, the lack thereof.

A teenager today faces the same basic insecurities that you and I once did at that age. They have a deep desire for acceptance, are very conscience about appearance, struggle with trust issues, and still hate to be told what to do. Some of this is hormonal (for both boys and girls) and some of it is developmental, yet all of it is characteristic of teens from any of the past few generations. Without an abundance of outside influences, raising a teenager is hard enough; yet leading a 21st century teenager is like trying to keep a cat still in a feather shop with ceiling fans.

If I could define the culture today in one world, it would be "I." Individualism is the marinade that our current society soaks in. From personal computers and personal trainers to "i" pods, pads, and phones, this is a very individualized world. It is no wonder that the 2013 Word of the Year was "Selfie."[1] A selfie, as I'm sure you know, is a personal picture an individual can easily take thanks to the front view camera on a smartphone. Today, selfies are the most popular way to take a picture with someone, or just of yourself. Oprah Winfrey even claimed that, now, taking a selfie with a celebrity is much more popular than getting their autograph.[2] Times have changed.

But "selfie" does not just describe a self-taken picture, for looking deeper we find that the word characterizes so much more than that. An individualist culture creates individuals, and our teenagers are engrossed in that identity. Even though, to their core, teenagers desire relationships, long for encouragement, live for community, and hope for love, there is a powerful force within them (and in many of us too) that makes them want to close down, shut out, plug in, and close up. This is nothing new. The same could have been said about my generation or yours. The main difference is that today's kids have the tools, toys, and resources to go deeper into the world of "I" and no tool is more useful in this case than that of social media.

The 21st Century Glass House

Living in a glass house has always meant that people should not criticize others for faults that they have themselves. But, I want to take that analogy and bring it into a new era of meaning. For the purpose of this conversation, glass house living represents a sense of privacy that is very public. If someone actually lived in a house with glass walls, they might still feel secure and private, just as living in a typical house might feel, yet they would not be hidden at all. They might feel free to dress how they want, say or do whatever they please, because they feel safe at home. Yet, all the while, everyone else can see them through the glass walls of their house. This is what life in the world of social media is truly like; living in a house of glass, because social media is a private world lived in the open.

As you can imagine, there would be a few major problems with living in a glass house, and those same problems exist in today's world of social media:

Everyone sees what you are doing. When the walls are made of glass, there is no privacy. When life is lived online, the same can be true. Later in this book we will examine ten of the most popular social media sites that teenagers are drawn to and how they can expose all sides of a teenager's life, development, and insecurities.

Thrown rocks can cause cracks. This takes us back to the original meaning of glass houses. When a rock is thrown at a house of glass, it creates a problem as the integrity of the house becomes weaker. Such can be the case with social media for kids. Cyberbullying is a very common problem online among teenagers, as is the public display of what would otherwise be a private matter. Kids are going to have relationship struggles. Best friends will always get into fights and dating couples will continue to break up, but today, those spats can easily become displayed publicly for everyone to see. This reality can often leave a mark; a crack in the glass of an already insecure, vulnerable teenage life.

Cracks are difficult to mend. Think about a fight or a breakup you might have had as a teenager, then think about how it might have felt for the other person to share the details, with a few hundred friends, of that which was never meant to be public. Or, maybe you did something embarrassing as a kid and it was then talked about or recorded for all to see. That takes an already hurtful situation and magnifies it. As the old adage states: "Sticks and stone may hurt my bones, but words will never hurt me."[3] Those words have never been true, but today they are painfully inaccurate as words are publicly thrown at unstable glass house lives.

But cracks are not only caused by rocks being thrown at glass houses; sometimes cracks occur by a rock thrown from within the glass house. Every glass house comes equipped with an identity generator. This is a shiny little thing that helps the individual appear better than they think they really are. Most social media platforms require users to create a profile. This is an online identity, yet it goes further than just a picture and a bio. Social media helps a user display whatever they want to portray about themselves. Like a model on the cover of a fashion magazine, flaws can be erased and a new identity can be generated to assure others that they have it all together. The temptation is to put up images that reflect how an individual wants others to see them, causing that person to begin believing it as well. This damage is internal and rarely becomes realized as an individual grows up pretending to be something that they are not. They come across as someone who is healthy, secure, wise, successful, and accomplished, when in reality, they are causing cracks from within that are causing the infrastructure of the life inside to crumble.

This description is certainly not the only result of social media. In fact, social media can be a really good thing when used in a healthy way. Like the Internet as a whole, one has to learn how to use it and how not to abuse it because it is only a tool, but a powerful one at that.

The Obvious, & Not-So Obvious, Dangers of Social Media

Social media has many good features: communication, creativity, and cultural awareness, just to name a few. Many of us who are active on social media find it to be fulfilling and fun. Yet, there are a number of known dangers of social media such as cyberbullying, online predators, and the sharing of inappropriate content, just to name three. With that said, there are many other dangers that are not commonly realized when a child is introduced to social networking. Here are a few:

Unhealthy Identity Issues - We all want to be liked, and many people are so dependent on the validation of acceptance that social media can feed that need or drain it in an instant. The number of followers/ friends, likes, re-posts, and comments all validate an insecure person's self-perception. Likewise, the ever-present cultural standards that are exaggerated online cause kids and adults alike to chase a dream to be something they are not. As you will learn later in this book, trends and hashtags are two important features of social media. A hashtag is a word or phrase preceding the pound symbol (#). Once that hashtag is used millions of times, it becomes a trend. Some of the most popular trends for teenage girls on social media are #thighgap, #thinspiration, #skinny, and #thinspo (short for "thinsporation"). For teens, hashtags are often a cry for help or a need for acceptance. Social media has become a stage for kids to find a voice and seek validation for the identity they so desperately want to become.

Unhealthy Community Involvement - Social media is just that, social. Well, kind of. Social media is social in the same way that someone can be in a room full of people and still be lonely. Having a following of "friends" in social media does not mean that someone has a real following of friends. This can be seen manifested in many ways. The truth is, online relationships rarely go deeper than just below the surface. For example, someone might post about what they had for dinner last night and someone else would comment about how good the picture looked. Then, both people will feel a deeper sense of friendship because they shared in such a great conversation about food. There are things people will say to others online that they would never say face to face. One person might dive deep into struggles and convictions with someone they don't even know, while another will chat with someone for years without developing the conversation at all. Everyone, especially a teenager, needs to have healthy friend relationships that can continue online, rather than the other way around.

Unhealthy Time Usage - Social media can be an

incredible time waster. It is fine to spend some time on Twitter and posting to Instagram, but when the time invested becomes obsessive, there is a problem. Most teenagers do not know how to manage time and therefore tend to spend too much "screen time" socializing, sometimes with people they don't even know. According to one study by the Kaiser Family Foundation, kids ages 8-18 spend, on average, seven and a half hours a day on media devices.[4] For a kid who is only awake for 12-16 hours a day, this is extraordinary.

Super Powers

When I was a kid, I dreamed that I had super powers. I could rule the world with strength, speed, and power. Today, kids still dream of many things, and the powers available to them are super powerful in a real way. Today, if a kid is talented enough, he can make a music video that can be seen by one million people. Likewise, if she is considered attractive enough, a female can go in her room, lock her door, take a topless selfie, and post it to certain websites that can be rated by thousands in a matter of hours. For a dating couple, a breakup can spread around the whole student body in minutes, and a hateful comment can be sent in a cowardly fashion without ever having to witness the person's reaction of hurt. Like the tools in Batman's belt, a cell phone, tablet, and computer connected to the world can bring instant fame or social shame in the matter of a few minutes. Our tech tools give us super powers, and we need to know how to handle them.

In July of 2014, a Nebraskan teenager named Tom saw

Paul McCartney and Warren Buffett sitting on a park bench outside a local ice cream shop in Omaha where Buffett lives. He took a selfie with McCartney and Buffett behind him and tweeted it. The next morning, Sir Paul himself re-tweeted it and the picture was then seen by millions and picked up by news publications all over the world.

In both the classic and modern versions of Spiderman, Peter Parker had to learn how to use his new super powers for good. In each rendition, he had to teach himself to fly using the web shooting from his veins. At first he fell, but eventually he understood how to handle it, and then used his powers to make a difference. In order for our kids to become responsible members of this society, they must learn to use the powers they have been given for good. Ironically, like Spiderman, we too have a "web" to learn to maneuver through, yet, in our case, the web has not become who we are, but instead it is just a tool on our very powerful belt (or maybe just in our pocket).

NOTES:

_____

_____

_____

_____

_____

CHAPTER 2
SOCIAL MEDIA 101

"Just as we teach our children how to ride a bike, we need to teach them how to navigate social media and make the right moves that will help them. The physical world is similar to the virtual world in many cases. It's about being aware. We can prevent many debacles if we're educated." *Amy Jo Martin, author & founder of Digital Royalty*

When writing about such a broad topic to a very broad audience, I decided that I needed to start at the very beginning so that no one gets left behind. As someone who has been working with teenagers for over 20 years, and somewhat of a self-proclaimed computer junkie myself, I sometimes falsely assume that adults know more about social media than they do. But, as I have worked alongside other adults my age and even younger who do not understand the basics, I realize that we are possibly further behind than one might think.

If you are reading this book, you most likely have kids that are either tweenagers (8-12) or teenagers (13-19). I am right there with you. One of the many challenges for the parents of these young people is trying to understand the world our children live in. Some parents throw up their hands and just say, "I'll never understand." Some might even confess that they shouldn't try, believing that a parent is not supposed to understand "their world." But I say that you should try, and that you should try very hard to understand the world that your kids are living in so that you are better equipped to relate to them and to help them understand how to live responsibly in that world. It is from that perspective that I am writing to you. With that said, let me call this class to order. Students, this is Social Media 101. If you do not think you should be in this class, you need to think again.

Raising Social Media Moguls

Unless you are unlike most parents of teens or pre-teens, it is probably safe to say that your child knows more about social media than you do. You might have been on Facebook for longer, and could possibly have more friend contacts than they do, but your kids may still know more about social media than you think they do. Why? Because this is their world. As a matter of fact, many of you are unknowingly raising social media moguls.

The reason that kids know a lot about these sites is that it has become socially necessary for them to know about them. Here are a few important points for you to know as a parent of a social media user.

• Facebook and Twitter are just a single drop in the

bucket of the social media options available to kids today. If you think, based on your own Facebook use, that at worst social media is a slight distraction to users, you don't understand the influence that social media has on kids.

- Kids use social media differently than adults do. For most adults it is a means of gaining information and keeping up with friends. To kids, it is a social and emotional lifeline connected to that individual's identity and self-esteem. Social Media is a very integral part of the teenage psyche.

- Most parents are out of the loop on standard social media usages, language, and dangers. Parents think that if they simply keep an eye on their child's Facebook wall, that they are protecting their child from social media issues.

- Social media is constantly changing as new platforms are being developed, and a parent needs to stay up on all the new advancements and know how to lead their children through it.

- Kids can be trustworthy, smart, and obedient in normal life and still find themselves in harmful and compromising positions online. The reason for this is that they often do not understand these dangers themselves, or they underestimate the dangers they are aware of.

We need to accept that social media is not going away; as a matter of fact, the opposite is true. Likewise, we need to understand that we should not simply forbid our children from using social media, either. This world is our new normal. Kids that are not completely versed in social media will be at a severe disadvantage throughout their lives, in higher education and career opportunities. So we cannot avoid it, nor can we afford not to protect them from it; therefore, we need to understand it so that we can lead them through it.

What is Social Media?

I told you we were starting from the beginning. Social media consists of a website or online application that allows for interaction and networking. Different from a typical website that just provides information, a social media site requires communication and the sharing of content in order to operate. Called the Web 2.0, social media has changed the way the internet is used. Take two of the world's most popular websites: Google and Facebook. One, as you probably know, is a social media site while the other is not. Google is a search engine. You type in something you want to find and Google gives you a list of online sources as an answer. There is no interaction between parties. Facebook, on the other hand, is a platform for you to converse with "friends," share thoughts, pictures, and let everyone know that the sandwich you had for lunch was the best you've ever eaten. A social media site will allow the user to create a profile (online identity), post statements and comments, share pictures and/or videos, send messages, and invite others to join and become friends or followers.

Currently, there are approximately 200 active websites

and apps characterized as social media sites. These are not all for kids, and not all are potentially harmful. Some are platforms very similar to networking sites like Facebook, and many are sites that neither you nor your kids would ever want to go on. Others are specific for certain social groups, particular countries, or niche networks and markets. In the next chapter of this book, I will share with you ten major social media platforms that are popular with kids and potentially dangerous if used recklessly.

So, how is a social media site dangerous, you might ask? Think about it in this way. Driving a car is not a dangerous act, in and of itself. You and I do it every day. Cars are built safely and the task of driving is not extremely difficult. But, what if a five-year-old was driving the car, would that scenario change? Even a safe vehicle with a basic operation is almost impossible for a five-year-old who lacks the mental, physical, and logistical development needed to drive a car. Even if you showed him how to start the car and put it in drive, the child would still have a wreck within seconds due to an inability to steer straight. In a similar way, teenagers know basic social media operations, but steering straight remains a major problem. This translates into kids not being cautious enough about the necessary responsibility it takes to maneuver the vehicle of social media.

According to the Pew Research Center's Internet, Science, and Tech division, teens are sharing a lot of very private and personal information. The 2013 Teens, Social Media, and Privacy study revealed that 91% of teenagers share photos of themselves online,

while 24% share personal videos. The study also showed that:
92% share their real name
84% post their personal interests
82% give their birthday
71% tell the city they live in
71% post the school they attend
62% share a relationship status
53% publicly post their email address
20% give out their phone number online

Some of this information is obviously more sensitive than others and some is more protected online than others, but all is available if the wrong person gets friended or followed.

Understanding How Social Media Works

Like many adults, you understand the basics of social media because you have a personal Facebook, Twitter, and/or Instagram account (the three most popular). But in an effort to catch everyone up, here is a basic overview of how social media works. In all cases, a social media site is designed to communicate with others, but just how and why that happens is often the main distinction. In most cases, a profile is created where the user will have a username, give some verifying information, and then be known by that identity, or avatar. These sites allow you, a user, to view the profile of other users. In most cases, you then have to friend or follow a particular user to gain access to more personal content. On Facebook or Linkedin, a popular business-related networking site, users must get permission to gain this access, whereas on sites like Twitter, a user can be followed without confirmation.

Once you are set up on a profile-based site, you typically have a wall or timeline that records your posted and shared content. Depending on one's settings, that content can be viewed by other users of the service. Once you have posted something on your timeline/wall/page, other people can "like" or "favorite" it, which means that they have seen and approved of what you shared. This is the payoff for many who seek validation for their online popularity. For specific usage rules for a social media platform, see my report on the top ten sites for kids in the next chapter of this book. In the back of this book is an in-depth glossary of social media terms that will be helpful as you read through the next section of this book. You might even want to read through the glossary before starting the next chapter.

Understanding The Power of the Hashtag

For teenagers and even college students, a hashtag can be the most important part of the comment. As mentioned at the end of the last chapter, a hashtag is a word or phrase (without spaces) preceding the pound (#) symbol. Using this in many social media platforms like Twitter, Facebook, and Instagram will create a link of that hashtag and connect it to other tweets and posts using the same tag. But, what might have started as an organizational tool has turned into a secondary way to communicate. A hashtag can be like the adjective to a noun, the punchline to the joke, or a surrender flag to the fight. Furthermore, a hashtag is a link to making a tweet or post more popular and noticed.

Here are a few examples of how that works. I love music, and U2 has been my all-time favorite band since the mid-80's. If I were to listen to classic U2 and wanted to share that on Twitter, I might write: "Enjoying some #JoshuaTree this afternoon on #iTunesRadio. #U2 #IveFoundWhatImLookingFor." So, everyone who followed me on Twitter would see this tweet and, since my personal Twitter account is linked to my Facebook account, my Facebook friends would see it, too. I included four hashtags in this post, and all four of them become a link for others to see as well. Hashtag-U2 might be the most common of the ones I wrote. Therefore, anyone in the world who clicks a #U2 will see a list with mine included, and since U2 is almost always a Trending Topic, there will always be the chance for people to like, favorite, share, or retweet my statement. (Usually when I tweet about U2, one or more U2 fan clubs and groups repost my statement, which opens up my little comment to potentially millions of people). The same can be true for the Hashtag- Joshua Tree (which is a popular U2 record from 1987) and Hashtag-iTunes Radio which is a free streaming feature of iTunes. The last tag I created was different. I do not expect the phrase Hashtag-I've Found What I'm Looking For to ever be trending or even repeated. I did that to be funny. In case you don't know, one of the most popular songs on The Joshua Tree album is called "I Still Haven't Found What I'm Looking For." For anyone who might see my tweet and get the pun, I was saying that I found what I was looking for by listening to U2.

Kids use hashtags in a similar way. In the back of this book I have included a short index of common and popular hashtags. Most of them are listed because they are a sign that the user might be seriously dealing with a problem and possibly crying out for help. The others in the list serve to define some abbreviations in case you see those online. Kids sometimes use hashtags to say things publicly that they would never say to an adult. For example, a simple Twitter search of the tag #selfinjury brings up many cries for help. One teen posted: "I think one of the things with cutting for me is about cutting out the parts of myself I don't like. #selfinjury." Another that I found is a little more subtle: "But Im Only Human #SelfInjury #Again." When seeing a hashtag like #suicidal, knowing the person is important to measure the seriousness of the statement. For example, a quick search of that hashtag gave me this tweet: "Sick of living tbh #depressed #suicidal" (note: tbh stands for "to be honest" online). Another tweet that I found read: "Woke up late, boss is gonna kill me. #suicidal." This is why knowing the person will give so much more clarity as to the seriousness of the hashtag. Regardless, there is always a level of reason for a hashtag. As a matter of fact "#hashtag" was created and is popular because, as they say, you always need a hashtag and if you can't think of one you simply use Hashtag-hashtag.

What Parents Need to Know

Before I introduce you to each of the ten sites listed in

chapter three, let's explore a list of 10 things that parents need to know about social media.

1. Dangerous people hang out on these sites, often posing as teenagers, hoping to meet up with naive users. Though not always the case, this is something to make kids aware of. People may not be who they appear to be in an online profile.

2. Despite popular thought, all pictures posted online potentially live forever. No one knows how long these sites will last and what would happen if they went off-line, but people can easily save a picture to their personal hard drive and, at any time, repost using another source.

3. Posted content (text, video, and pictures) can be seen by people a user is not directly connected to. Using Facebook for example, depending on a user's settings, a friend of a friend can see pictures, and anything that is shared (re-posted) can be seen by all friends of the one who shared it (and so on).

4. Posted content can be found by something called the Rabbit Hole Effect. This occurs when someone in a site like Facebook or Instagram sees a picture, for example, of a friend or follower. Then they click on the link which might take the person to a comment or post from a friend of your friend. Then another link will take that individual to another user, and so on, until the person is 5+ relationships deep, viewing content from someone they may or may not know, yet are not connected with online.

5. The Children Online Privacy Protection Act restricts social media sites from allowing profile users under the age of 13. If you have a child under the age of 13 with a Facebook or Instagram profile, for example, they are breaking this federal law. Some social media platforms, like Twitter, do not ask an age when setting up a profile, yet this does not mean that they allow tween users. According to Facebook, there are 3.6 million underage users per month and, in 2011, over 20,000 underage accounts were shut down daily.

6. Social media is not just a place for fun interactions for teens; it is where real relationships develop. According to one statistic, 35% of teenagers argue with friends via social media, often without parents even knowing about it, and 20% end friendships because of interactions on social media.[5]

7. Cyber-bullying is a real thing. Fifty-two percent of young people claim to have been subjected to some level of bullying online, while 95% of teenagers admit that they have witnessed cyber-bullying and ignored the behavior.[6] Online abuse can occur from the public sharing of personal information or images, posting threatening comments towards someone, making untrue accusations online, etc.

8. Teenagers are notorious about hiding their identity online through fake or secondary secret profiles. According to ContentWatch, a leading parent online control software company, 70% of

teenagers hide their online behavior.[7] That same survey discovered that 48% of teens look up answers to tests online, 36% access sexual topics, 32% look up pornographic images, and 31% download pirated music and movies. Meanwhile, 77% of parents says that they are not concerned with their child cheating online and 74% are trusting that their teen is not seeking age-inappropriate online content.

9. Social media can become a media addiction, just like gaming, television, and other apps. Teenagers become obsessed with who is doing what and get to a point where they cannot function more than a few minutes without checking in online. This level of social interaction produces unhealthy and unrealistic relationship realities.

10. Many teenagers do not understand that their social media activity can affect college entrance and scholarships as well as future job opportunities because those agencies are screening social media sites looking for signs of the individual's character. This is not something that a high school student is thinking about when he/she posts something carelessly on spring break that might keep them from getting a job after high school.

Many of these ten points will be discussed again throughout the remainder of this book. It is important to understand that social media is a powerful tool that can be used either safely and effectively, or carelessly and dangerously. Your kids need to know the difference, and you, the parent, need to know more about the world of social media.

NOTES:

_____

_____

_____

_____

_____

_____

_____

_____

_____

_____

_____

_____

_____

_____

_____

_____

_____

CHAPTER 3
TEN POPULAR SOCIAL MEDIA SITES FOR TEENAGERS

"The problem with social media is there is too much freedom. It's too much, too young." *Cara Delevingne, actress, model, and singer*

In this chapter we will examine ten of the most popular social media sites for kids. These sites are mostly share sites, meaning that teenagers are posting content for others to see. Most of them require a profile, but not all of them have restrictions about who can see that profile. For each site, I will explain how it works, what attracts teens to it, how the privacy settings work, and the dangers to watch out for. I will present them in the order that I believe they are the most popular to kids. The exact order of popularity is not incredibly important, but it will give you an idea of the likelihood that your child may know or even use the site.

There are many social media and other interactive formats that will not be examined in this list. One of the most common is texting. Even though one of the ten highlighted sites is a text messaging app, mobile phone texting is not technically a social media platform. But it is important to know that it is one of the most common forms of tech-communication by teenagers today. The truth is, kids can get in as much trouble with texting as they can with some of these social networking sites. Sexting is a huge issue with teenagers, yet this act can be utilized on almost every one of the sites presented in this chapter. The point of this particular book is not necessarily to address behavior, but rather to educate parents on the various platform available to kids to act out such behavior. Inappropriate behavior is a deeper, heart issue that will not get better just by taking away a device or deleting an app. Along with texting, I will not be reviewing social media sites like Google+, Linkedin, or Pinterest, because they are not very popular with teenagers; Pandora, iTunes, or Beats, because they are technically not social media platforms; and Buzzfeed or Funny or Die because, though interactive, they are secondary share-only websites that work within primary platforms like Facebook and Twitter.

For the remainder of this chapter, I will lay out ten of the most common social media sites for teenagers. It is important to note that this is far from an exhaustive list, and only includes platforms that were popular when this book was written. For each platform, I will describe what it does, how to use it, and give some concerns that parents should know about.

The following are the ten social media profiles that will be presented and explained in this chapter: Instagram, Facebook, Youtube, Twitter, Snapchat, Tumblr, Ask.fm, Kik Messenger, Yik Yak, and Whisper.

Instagram

www.instagram.com
Launched in 2010

Instagram is a social networking site that allows users to post photos and videos and then share that media with Instagram followers, as well as on other social media platforms like Facebook, Twitter, and Tumblr. The most unique feature of an Instagram picture is the distinctive square shape and variety of digital filters than can be added to the image. Instagram videos are limited to 15-seconds in length. Kids often prefer Instagram as their default photo sharing platform because it cuts right to the chase of photo and video sharing, as opposed to something like Facebook that also includes links, status updates, and product ads.

Instagram is one of the most popular social media site for teenagers, and is rated as the site with the most engaged users.[8] Kids like Instagram because it combines all the best social media features for teens: sharing, liking, and commenting. Instagram is mainly a mobile app platform, and though available on the website, it is limited. Instagram is now owned by Facebook.

Signing-Up & Using Instagram

To sign up, one must download the mobile app and create a profile. Once signed-in, a new user can add a profile picture and a short bio description. Users can browse some photos in the general public as well as those of people they follow. Users can also comment on a photo in a chat-like function. Photos and videos on Instagram are public by default, meaning that anyone can see them without approval. This setting can be changed if the user knows how, if he/she even wants to. To create a private account, a user needs to click "Privacy" and select the option to make photos private. Once this is done, only approved followers can view pictures and videos posted by that user.

Settings and Notifications

A user can adjust the settings so that they can control the access and activity on their Instagram feed. This can include everything from allowing someone to post comments and share media, as well as tagging (linking a user to a picture) or adding someone to what is called a Popular page. The Notification setting will alert users when any of these things have been done. Instagram posts can also link to Facebook, Twitter, or a variety of other social media sites for more visibility. It will then be up to the settings of that platform as to how that picture or video is shared, liked, or commented on.

Instagram Concerns for Parents

- Due to the public default setting, Instagram can easily show inappropriate (but not pornographic) photos and videos.

- Instagram has a lot of underage users who have lied about their age to qualify. All social media outlets are required by law to only admit users who are 13 years of age and older, but none require proof. Underage usage is a problem across all social networking platforms, but since Instagram is one of the most popular with kids, it has the largest underage usage rate.

- Unless an account is marked as private, any user, friend or stranger, can view all of the pictures in an Instagram account. This can reveal private and personal information such as where someone lives, where they go to school, and who they may be related to or friends with.

Other Similar Services

One app that is growing and could one day overcome Instagram and Twitter for kids is Pheed (www.pheed.com). This is a social media app that allows users to post text, pictures, or videos that can be liked or followed. This site has the same basic conceptual structure as Instagram, but with more media options to share. The main difference from any other social media platform is that the user can charge a fee to view the content. The hope of the developers is that celebrities will begin using the service and post original content that kids will then pay to see. That has not happened yet.

Facebook

www.facebook.com
Launched in 2004

Facebook is known as the quintessential social media site, as it is the world's most popular social networking platform. With that said, it is no longer the premiere networking site for teenagers, largely because too many adults are on it. Facebook is a network made of "friends." Once a profile is created, a user begins friending people they know, yet it is not until those friend requests are accepted that the connection is made. Once two people are Facebook friends, they can write on each other's wall, tag photos, and chat (instant message). Teenagers who still use Facebook use it because it is what they know and it is where most of their personal connections remain. Many teens use Facebook as a public site to post pictures and make comments that are pleasing to parents and other adults, then use more private sites for their day-to-day interactions with peers.

There are three main parts to a personal Facebook page: Profile, News Feed, and Message. The profile is the personal page that all users create when they set up their account. It features their name, picture, and any information that the user wants to give out, which can include schools attended, jobs worked, family members on Facebook, relationship status, likes, hobbies, favorite movies and music, etc. Once a user posts a status update, picture, link, or video, it appears on the person's Timeline. The News Feed is the main page of Facebook and serves as a commons area for one's friend's posts to show up for viewing. Depending on settings and history, some friends' content appears more often on the News Feed than others. Message is how users communicate privately on Facebook. Just like an email, a user can send a message to one or more friends, and if that friend is logged in, they will receive it instantly.

Signing Up for Facebook

Signing up to get a Facebook account is done on the website, and is a pretty quick process. First, you enter in basic information and then you will be given a chance to put in as many personal details as you want to provide. The options will include everything from school and work details to relationship status, personal info such as city, state, email, and phone number, and type of hobbies, music, and movies that an individual might like. A user can choose the information they want to display, and anything that is left blank will not be included in the profile. The next step is to adjust the privacy and notification settings.

Settings and Notifications

Facebook privacy and notification settings will help the user determine how public or private they would like to be on Facebook. This will affect everything from who can see posts, who can comment on them, and how a user can be contacted. Facebook allows a user to be as selective as they want to be. A Facebook user can restrict certain people from seeing particular posts or create groups that will be the only ones to see certain posts. It is a common practice for teenagers to have two groups, one with parents and other adult family members and one without. They then post semi-regularly to the parent group, yet are more active on the other. A user can also block other users from seeing or sending them posts, requests, and messages. All of these options are found in General Account Settings. Simply click the down arrow in the blue horizontal bar at the top of the website (the mobile app is very limited as far as setting changes), and click Settings.

Facebook Concerns for Parents

- The default privacy setting allows anyone to see pictures, friend lists, and some personal information, as well as authorizing Friends to see everything that has been posted. Make sure your child knows what settings need to be changed. Viewing the Activity Log in the settings tab will show everything that a user has shared on Facebook.

- Facebook can be linked to many other social media sites and posted/shared content can link to those other sites if they are set up to do so. This can become a problem if Facebook settings are set strictly but other linked sites are not.

- As with any photo-related social media site, users need to be aware that even though they do not personally post a picture of themselves, that does not mean someone else has not posted a picture with them in it. Furthermore, if a picture is posted and the individual is not tagged, they may not even know the photo has been made public until they are told about it. This can especially be concerning if the image shows inappropriate or questionable behavior.

- Under normal settings, Facebook allows users to

send a private message to someone they are not friends with. This can lead to stranger danger for young teens, as well the passing of spam-related links for all users.

Other Similar Services

Another service that was intended to rival Facebook is Google+. The main difference is, instead of having "friends," a user creates "circles" which gives them more control as to what they share and who sees it. For parents, this means that teens can form closed online groups to communicate and share content. Google+ is still not as popular with teenagers as the other platforms mentioned in this book.

Youtube
www.youtube.com
Launched in 2005

Youtube is a video sharing social media site that allows users to upload, view, and comment on videos. An individual does not have to register as a user to watch videos on Youtube, but will need an account to post a video for others to see. YouTube is now owned by Google.

A registered user can create a Youtube channel and other users can follow that channel. Then, once the channel creator posts another video to that particular channel, the followers are notified. Even though a minimum age of 13 is required to create an account, any individual can watch the posted videos. Videos considered to contain offensive material are restricted only to users who designate themselves as over 18 years of age.

What started as a site for amateur video sharing now includes professionally filmed videos, trailers, and advertisements. Today, most artists and athletes, organizations and causes, corporations and products all have Youtube channels, allowing viewers to watch just about anything online for free. To cover these costs, many Youtube videos begin with a commercial that cannot be skipped until allowed.

<u>Signing Up for Youtube</u>
Sign-up is easy, and can be done with just an email address and password. Since Youtube is owned by Google, a Google account can be used as a Youtube

account. Users are asked about their age, but proof is not required.

Youtube Settings
Since one does not need an account unless posting a video, making a comment, or following a channel, Youtube settings are only used for posted videos. These settings allow the user to make the video public, private, or unseen by a search. Youtube does have a Safety mode for younger kids that will screen out potentially obscene content. If a parent needs to know what videos a child is watching, they can look at the viewed history list in the settings (you would need to be logged in as them).

Youtube Concerns for Parents
• The main concern with Youtube is the access to videos that you would normally not want your child to view. Whether it is bad language, sexual content, or just questionable behavior, there is very little that an individual can't find on Youtube, with or without an account. Nudity is very prominent on Youtube. If a search leads to a sexually explicit site, a warning pops up and requires the user to check a box authorizing that they are older than 18 years old. There is no other verification needed to access those videos.

• Video comments often carry a vulgar overtone. There are many people who make comments on Youtube that are completely unrelated to the video. Some users use this opportunity to advertise about something, make general rude comments, or even get into conversations with others on the comment feed. Youtube rarely, if ever, steps in to stop this activity.

Other Similar Services

Another popular video platform, called Vine, loops video footage up to six seconds, showing it over and over. This video can then be shared on Twitter or Facebook. The only concern for kids is the content and intent of the video that is shared.

Twitter

www.twitter.com
Launched in 2006

Twitter is a microblogging and social media network that allows users to send out short messages consisting of 140 characters or less. These short texts are called "Tweets." Registered users can send and read Tweets, and unregistered users can read them unless an account is marked as private.

Twitter has become the premier social media platform for celebrities, companies, organizations, and anyone else wanting to be seen and heard. A Twitter account can be used to share simple thoughts, links, and quotes from famous sources, etc. There are also many "fake" accounts that share anecdotes that would be funny if that person truly said them. Some people, especially celebrities, are known to have millions of Twitter followers.

The Hashtag became popular in social media through Twitter, as it is used to highlight a word with special meaning. A re-posting of a Tweet is called a "Retweet," and a Tweet that gets Tweeted and Retweeted over and over can become a Trending Topic. A Twitter user can click on a Hashtag to view other mentions of that word (even by those they don't follow) as well as Trending Topics. Twitter has made the world a little bit smaller due to the chance someone famous can see and even retweet a post of a follower.

Signing Up for Twitter

Just like with the other sites mentioned, signing up for a Twitter account is very easy and only takes a name, email address, and an original Twitter handle/username. As with most social media accounts, email verification is necessary before an account becomes active. Twitter no longer asks for a birthdate for age verification, like Facebook and Instagram do.

Settings and Notifications

Once a user is verified via email, the account is active and they are ready to Tweet. The profile page can be updated with a picture, a background, and a bio so others can know who the person is. Settings also include restrictions about followers and the option to be a private account where only followers can see Tweets. Notifications include email and app messages that are sent when someone Tweets or Retweets the user. Twitter does have private message capabilities, but users can not send a private message to someone who is not following them.

Twitter Concerns for Parents

- Due to the wide use of celebrities and others in culture, Tweets can be explicit in nature. A teenager will likely follow the musicians they like and the sports and TV stars they admire. Those Tweets are not censored the way comments made on television would be.

- Twitter is a fast-response public messaging tool, meaning that an individual can be angry and send something without thinking and never be able to unsay it. High school and college students have been kicked out of schools because of threatening or inappropriate Tweets.

- Tweets, Retweets, and numbers of followers can become a popularity mark and status symbol for kids, which can be unhealthy if the individual places too much value on it.

- Unlike Facebook where "friends" have to mutually accept each other, Twitter users can follow someone without the other person knowing who they are. This can allow one user to keep up with another without the followed user being aware.

- Tweets are able to go viral more easily than Facebook posts, and Tweets are the only social media content that is logged in the Library of Congress, meaning that Tweets live on forever.[9]

Snapchat

www.snapchat.com
Launched in 2011

Snapchat is a photo messaging site that allows users to send pictures (usually selfies) and video clips with added text to a selected recipient via the Snapchat mobile app. These sent pictures and clips are known as Snaps. The sender can set the image to be visible for a selected amount of time (from 1 to 10 seconds) before it disappears and becomes hidden from the receiver's device. Snapchat has a number of features that are unique to this platform. First, you can only share content privately. There is no public wall or Timeline for Snapchat. Secondly, the content is not available to the user after it is hidden.

Different from Snaps, Snapchat Stories is a collection of images that a user can share over a 24-hour period to a group of chosen friends. This group of pictures and/or video last longer than normal Snaps, but then disappear after the 24-hour period is over. Snap Messaging gives the user the ability to send a Chat, which is like a text message, to another approved user. Once the message has been sent and received, it will disappear just as Snaps do, but not before the recipient can save info in the message if desired. This feature also allows users to take part in live video chats.

In January 2015, Snapchat introduced Discover, which allows companies and brands to display Snapchat Stories for users to experience. A user can click on Discover and see a variety of popular logos from television networks and products, and then watch a predetermined clip. These Discover Stories change daily. Snapchat has yet another new feature called Snapcash, where one user can send money to another from their debt card simply by typing the "$" and an amount, then pressing the on-screen Snapcash button. Transfer fees do apply.

Signing Up for Snapchat
Signing up is as easy as downloading the mobile app, clicking "Sign-up" and entering a name, email address, and verifying a birth date. After these steps, the new user will pick a password and then is ready to begin adding contacts and sending Snaps. As with other social media sites, contacts can be added quickly by allowing Snapchat to scan your phone and online contacts for other Snapchat accounts.

Sending A Snap
To send a snap, the user will push the center round button at the bottom of the screen, which will enable the device's camera. Once the picture or video has been taken, the user will have the option to save the media to the phone. This option will not be available once the Snap has been sent. The next step is to select the time limit that the Snap will be shown, from 1 to10 seconds. The sender then gets the option to add text to the picture or even draw something on it. After, the Snap is ready to send.

Receiving A Snap
The recipient will be notified of a new Snap and told how much time it is set for it to be seen. The viewer must hold down their finger on the screen for the Snap to continue through the duration. Then the user

has the opportunity to select a replay. The replay feature must be selected before the Snap comes through, and will only replay a Snap from the past 24 hours. Also, a user can only replay one Snap in a 24 hour period.

Snapchat Concerns for Parents
- The most obvious concern is that Snapchat gives a child permission to do something indecent without a fear of getting caught. Snaps are notorious for being inappropriate pics sent to tease another user. This is arguably why Snapchat is the most popular free app downloaded from the Apple Store. According to one website that ranks apps, it boasts: "Hands down, Snapchat is the best app to use if you want to send naughty pictures to someone. Every picture or short video message you send deletes itself forever after about 10 seconds."[10]

- Snapchat originally stated that once a Snap disappears, it was deleted and gone, but that did not seem to be the case. After a 2014 investigation, the Federal Trade Commission proved that Snaps were actually stored on the company's server. Now, Snapchat reportedly no longer saves those images but no one can say for sure where they go. Bottom line, kids need to know that content sent online is never completely lost.

- A Snap image can be saved in a screenshot on the mobile device (holding down the "Home" and "Wake/Sleep" buttons on iPhone and iPad devices). This is the reason Snapchat requires a user to keep touching the screen to view a Snap for the entire time. This can still be done, but once a screenshot is taken, the sender will receive a notification. Users can get around this by viewing the Snap on one device (iPad) and taking a picture of the screen with another device (iPhone).

• There are a few new apps that have been developed to secretly save Snapchat photos and video, and all of them basically work the same. Once a user receives a notification of a new Snapchat message, that user will first open this other app before looking at the Snap. The secondary app will record and save the Snap message permanently. The five most common apps that do this are SnapBox, Snapchat Saver, SnapCrack, SaveMySnaps, and SnapSave.

Tumblr
www.tumblr.com
Launched in 2007

Tumblr is a microblogging and social media site that allows users to post multimedia content to a short-form personal blog page. A user can use these sites to post pictures, video, texts, content, or basically anything they want. What sets this apart from a common blog is that it is also a social network. Users can follow other blogs and share content. If a teenager is a big music fan, for example, he can follow all of the Tumblr sites of his favorite bands and fill the page with that content. Tumblr sites can be private, but typically are not. Users can tag content for easy search ability, as well as re-post content from other sites. There are currently over 100 million Tumblr blog sites.

Tumblr is not a protected site for kids. It is known to be riddled with spam requests, as well as pornographic material. Because platform users are the ones creating and sharing content, the views and perspectives shared are often harmful in nature. Tumblr does provide a "Safe Mode" for a user to select, but that option only filters out sites that are marked as displaying adult content, and the user of those sites must choose to flag themselves as such. Tumblr does not seem to be very concerned about the openness of its content, stating: "Sure. We have no problem with that kind of stuff. Go nuts. Show nuts. Whatever."[11] Tumblr is owned by Yahoo.

Setting-Up A Tumblr Page
Signing up for a Tumblr page is simple with a unique

username and email address. There are two options for Tumblr pages: creating content and copy content. Since this is a sharable page, users typically try to find content that would be sharable to others. This is how one gains followers. Content is either copied or shared from the Dashboard, which is an easy to use creation page. A user can search tags for content and use other social media following lists to find users to follow and be followed by.

Why is Tumblr So Popular?
At first glance, Tumblr seems to be popular because users can follow interesting people and repost funny comments, but that can also be done on other social media sites. The uniqueness of Tumblr is that it combines the self-expression of a blog and the crowded community of a social networking site. Many people feel that the problem with a blog is that it is hard to attract readers. Tumblr solves this problem by connecting all the content through tags and followings.

Tumblr Concerns for Parents
- Tumblr is known for being consumed with pornography. The site has very limited privacy control, meaning that almost anything goes on Tumblr. Sexually-explicit material is allowed on the site and even though porn video is not, users are allowed to link porn to their Tumblr page. This means that a user can search and find just about any degree of content easily and quickly.

- Even though federal law requires a social media user to be at least thirteen years of age, Tumblr does not ask for an age verification making it essentially open for any age. This is a concerning issue for a site with unrestricted content.

- A user can block another user who might be harassing them on the site, but that block only keeps the users from communicating and does not prevent the blocked user from viewing the blocker's page.

- One troubling result of Tumblr is that it is very easy to post content for all to see. When a user sees something interesting on a blog or website, they can click a "Share on Tumblr" button and post directly to their microsite. Tumblr also encourages collaborative blogging where two, ten, or even a hundred users can co-author a post together. This feature is attractive to kids who want to be a part of a group effort but could accidentally link themselves to content that is questionable in nature.

Other Similar Services

Wanelo, which stands for Want, Need, Love, is a social media platform that combines shopping, fashion blogging, and social networking in one app. Wanelo has become very popular with teens, allowing them to discover, share, and buy products that they like. The similarity with Tumblr is that a Wanelo user will fill a page with these items and interests for others to view and share.

Ask.fm

www.ask.fm
Launched in 2010

Ask.fm is a social media site that allows a user to pose a question, and others are able to post answers to the question. The site is very popular with kids all over the world and has more recently become very popular among teens in the United States. The comments on this site are not monitored by the company, and therefore the range of content includes all levels of behavior.

Cyberbullying is common on Ask.fm, as users will post a question or comment to specific individuals that threatens or disgraces them. In 2013, a 14-year-old girl in Great Britain committed suicide after being bullied on Ask.fm. In response, Prime Minister David Cameron asked parents in the U.K. to boycott this and other sites. Ask.fm replied by promising more security and privacy on the site, but nothing notable has been done.

Joining and Using Ask.fm
An individual can sign up on the site with a name and email address. Birth date verification is not used. Current users of Facebook, Twitter, Tumblr, and Google+ can use those sites to sign themselves up on Ask.fm. The next step is to find people to follow. Users can enter in names or email addresses to find people on the site. By following someone, a user can then see the questions and answers that person has answered. The site's main page features a live stream of Q&A's that a user can read and follow.   Ask.fm

operates in a similar way to Twitter with a moving feed of followers, yet questions and answers are anonymous. Alongside user-produced questions, Ask.fm also poses random questions to encourage interaction network-wide.

The Ask.fm settings allow the user to designate if their questions will be answered anonymously or by people they know, as well as blocking certain users from answering questions. Ask.fm is easily integrated onto Facebook and Twitter, meaning that a question can be posted on those sites when they are posted on the Ask.fm feed, allowing for more interaction.

Ask.fm Concerns for Parents
- There are no rules for what can be asked on this site; therefore a lot of inappropriate material is shared. Ask.fm states on its own website that the content is not monitored. There are a lot of topics communicated from light-hearted questions to questions that are abusive, bullying, and sexual in nature.

- My biggest concern is that a site like this makes everyone an expert with an answer, confusing kids with false truths. If an individual is seeking an important answer to a life question and has no one else to ask, they might post it on Ask.fm, allowing for users posting answers as a form of entertainment. Ask.fm is not a healthy alternative for counseling or accountability.

- If a kid is being harassed on the site, the bully can be blocked, but this option is not perfect. First, because this site uses anonymous profiles, the user may not ever know who is doing the bullying. Secondly, blocking a user does not prevent them from seeing the profile of the individual and all other interactions.

- This site is based in Latvia, a country in northern Europe, which is why it has less security and privacy.

Kik Messenger
www.kik.com
Launched in 2010

Kik Messenger is an instant message app that will send text, photos, videos, sketches, and more, all within the mobile app. Think about having an app exclusively for text messages, and you have Kik. The difference, and the advantage to some teens, is that Kik does not use a cell phone number, therefore a young teen who has an iPod Touch, for example, but not a cell phone, can use Kik. Kik is different from most social media platforms, and some might even say that it is not a social media network. Regardless, it is very popular and is included in this list because there are some important features that parents need to know about.

There are many other text messaging/ instant messaging apps available on the market. Facebook, Instagram, and Snapchat each have an IM feature. Also, there is another popular texting app called WhatApp (owned by Facebook) that works a lot like Kik, except for the fact that WhatApp requires a phone number and operates on the same type of technology as a text message.

Setting-Up A Kik Account
To start using Kik, an individual will first need to download the Kik mobile app, which is very versatile and available for most major mobile carriers. A new user will need a phone number or an email address to sign up. Once a username is created, the user is ready to use the service. Developing a list of contacts can be done from phone numbers, email addresses, or other

social media friends/followers lists, such as Facebook. A user will use either WiFi or data from a phone or tablet for the service.

<u>Kik Concerns for Parents</u>
- As with any social media platform, one of the biggest risks for parents is the potential for inappropriate material that can be seen by kids. In 2014, Kik scored a one out of seven points on Electronic Frontier Foundation's secure messaging scorecard. The reason for this is because of encryption issues that are not completely secure.

- As mentioned before, Kik does not require a phone number, which means anyone with an iPod Touch or iPad, or other tablet, can send text messages through Kik. It is important that parents realize this because, otherwise, an uninformed adult might assume that their younger child is not texting because he/she doesn't have a cell phone. This could also be a separate means of texting for a child who has had a phone taken away or wants to hide text conversations.

- Even though Kik is not a large public network, there can still be bullying and abuse, as well as sexting. A user can block other users on Kik. If a parent needs to look back at a history of messages to prove abuse, note that the app only stores the last 1000 messages per conversation for the past 48 hours and 500 older messages on Apple products, and 600 message per conversation in 48 hours and 200 for older messages on Android devices.

Other Similar Services

Another instant messaging app that is popular with teens is Oovoo. It allows for text, video, or audio chats up to 12 locations at once with HD quality video. This is a very popular app that is growing in usage, and if there was going to be an 11th platform on my top-10 list, it would be Oovoo. It is the hope of the developers that this app will replace Skype for teens, as they just announced in early 2015 that Oovoo will soon be available on the Playstation 4.

Yik Yak

www.yikyakapp.com
Launched in 2013

As they say, the most important three words in real estate are location, location, location. The same could be said about the social media site Yik Yak. This app gives users the ability to post comments anonymously that can be read by any other users within a 10-mile radius. The app uses the device's GPS location software and scrolls comments in a Twitter-like live feed. There is no registration needed for this app, allowing anyone to use the application.

Yik Yak is extremely popular with teenagers and college student for the very fact that they can interact with random people anonymously. Most of the comments on Yik Yak are of the most vulgar of levels, and the app is notorious for gossip, slander, and cyber bullying. The app also allows users to rank comments with an up or down arrow, fueling the sender to be as funny, rude, specific, or demeaning as possible. Think for a moment if you could publicly shout something, anything, without anyone knowing that it is you shouting. That is Yik Yak. This is the 21st-century version of writing a comment on the wall of a gas station bathroom stall. The app also gives the user the chance to peek into other cities, universities, or communities to view the comments begin posted. A peeking user cannot make comments or post a rating on posts that are not local.

Using Yik Yak
After downloading the app, Yik Yak triggers the GPS

on the device and pinpoints the exact location of the user. At this moment, the user sees the live feed of other users within a 10-mile radius. To post a Yak, a user touches the top right symbol and starts typing a comment that can be no more than 200 characters. The user can choose to add a handle (remember there is no registration) and then posts the Yak in real-time. Soon, depending on how populated the area is, others will begin to rate the comment. Other tabs on the app include "Peek," "Me" (seeing a list of the user's own Yaks), and "More," which allows a user to see top-ranked Yaks and other links.

Yik Yak Concerns for Parents

- Parents need to know that there is nothing good that can come from this app. It is bad news from beginning to end. As a matter of fact, after an excessive amount of harassment and bullying claims, the founders of the company put in a series of geofences (an online "fence" that disables the use of the app in designated areas) around all U.S. middle schools and high schools.

- If you live in a populated area, and especially within 10 miles of a college or university, the chatter on Yik Yak will be constant and your child will see every type of sexual comment and more. There is no filter for the app to only see "PG" material. It is all or nothing with Yik Yak.

- A common excuse that some teens like to give their parents for why they need to be on Yik Yak is that it can be used for informative purposes. There was a report of a snow storm at the University of

Alabama in 2014 which took out the extreme weather communication system, and students apparently used Yik Yak to communicate. The truth is, if the data and Wi-Fi services are working, Facebook, Twitter, and other online communicative tools would work just as well in this case. Typically, the most popular PSA that Yik Yak is credited with is warning people of police cars hiding near highways with a radar gun.

- Yik Yak is R-rated "entertainment". Nothing else. I can make an argument for almost all of the social media sites mentioned in this book with positive, useful characteristics, but not for Yik Yak. The anonymous feature makes this app pointless for building community, friendship, or learning anything useful. Yik Yak is pure gossip and cyber-bully central.

Other Similar Services

One app that is not necessarily like Yik Yak in concept but popular with college students is Omegle. Omegle is a video site that pairs two strangers up to have a conversation. They are anonymous by name, only calling them "You" and "Stranger 1." Like Yik Yak, this site does not require a user name. In 2014 the service offered a "Dorm Chat" feature where two individuals with .edu email accounts could be paired up to chat.

Whisper
www.whisper.sh
Launched in 2012

Whisper is a secret-sharing, confession-promoting app that allows users to anonymously share their deepest, darkest secrets online with an image to express the tone of the confession. The tagline for the app is "Express Yourself - Share Secrets - Meet New People." Whisper is rated 17+ by the Apple App Store for "Frequent/Intense Mature/Suggestive Themes."

A Whisper (the term for the posted secret) is a confession-based statement that is posted over a square stock photo that helps the viewer identify more with the statement. An example of a Whisper is a picture of cash falling and the words, "I'm a girl and have paid for every single date I have been on."[12] This app fools users into thinking that they are "letting it all out" or speaking to an understanding audience, when in reality, the readers are mostly just there for entertainment purposes.

How Whisper Works
After downloading and opening up the app, the new user is brought to a page with featured Whispers. The next step is to type in an anonymous Whisper confession. The app will then suggest a picture to lay the statement over, or the user can search for other options until one is selected. If a gallery picture is not selected, the user will have the option to pick one from his own mobile photo library or take a picture with the device's camera. The font of the text can also be changed before posting. The next step is to pick tags

so that the Whisper can be searched. For the one mentioned above, a tag like "dating" or "money" might be selected. The next step is to post the picture. If this is the first time a user has posted, a screen will pop up with a unique username suggestion, and a request for a PIN. This suggested username is meant to give the user total anonymity. From there, the user will be taken to the main page of the app where the Whisper will be viewable. The user will then have a chance to share on other social media platforms, which seems to me, at least, to go against the entire point of being anonymous. The user can check back on the post to see if others have "hearted" (liked) it or reposted the confession. This is where the "meet new people" component comes in.

When one goes to the site, there are categories of Whispers to consider viewing. They include: "Popular," "LOL," "Relationships," "OMG," "Faith," "LGBTQ," and "Animals."[13] There are also two main tabs labeled "Stories" and "Questions." The Stories are specific occurrences that a user can share about. Questions are simply questions a user can answer with a confession. A few examples of the stories one can read and write about are: "Times I Got Caught Having Sex," "First Kiss Confessions," "Embarrassing Stories About Sex In Dorm Rooms," "Drunk People Who Let Liquid Courage Lead The Way," and "Gamers Who Let Their Obsessions Get Out Of Control." One example in the Questions section is, "What is one thing that your family would be surprised to learn about you?" At the time I saw this question on the website, it had 5660 responses ranging from confessions of drug usage, sex, attempted suicides, secret homosexual behavior, self-harm, and the list goes on and on and gets worse and worse. The more obscene and harmful, the more hearts (likes) the comments got.

Whisper Concerns for Parents
- If a user has enabled the location service (GPS) on the device, this app will show a list of Whispers nearby to other users. This can create a potential harmful situation if a predator seeks out someone pretending to be a nearby helpful friend and arranges a meet-up through the reply section of the site.

- The site requires a PIN to view a past posting history, keeping parents or other concerned adults from seeing the secrets.

- There have been many reported bullying cases where kids have targeted another kid, or a teacher, and posted their name and something negative about that person. This can be an easy way to anonymously slander another person.

- Whisper claims to track users in order to prevent shady individuals from using the site (which is good), but this also means that users are not completely anonymous, at least to Whisper.

- It is hard to know if many of these confessions are true or shared for shock value, but either way, this site is turning confessions into content for entertainment. That is not healthy.

Other Similar Services

PostSecret is an older app that basically does the same thing as Whisper. It is not as trendy now, but is another confession-over-picture type service. PostSecret became famous in 2013 when someone posted "I said she dumped me, but, really, I dumped her (body)," and gave a link on a map to a park in Chicago. Police were called and they investigated, but nothing was found and it was deemed a hoax.[14]

NOTES:

_____

_____

_____

_____

_____

_____

_____

_____

_____

_____

CHAPTER 4
ONLINE RESPONSIBILITY &
SAFEGUARDS

"They haven't used it. We limit how much technology our kids use at home." *Steve Jobs, founder of Apple* (After being asked if his kids love the new iPad)

Social media is like a match. When it is lit it can give light to everyone in the room, or it can set fire to the house and burn it to the ground. The purpose of a match is to make fire, and the purpose of fire, well, that is up to the one striking the match. There are some places that we should never strike a match: near a dynamite store comes to mind. And there are certain people who should not play with fire: those who are too young to understand the danger that it can cause.

Likewise, there are some social media platforms that everyone should stay away from, and there are some people who should stay away from social media. As parents, it is up to us to know the difference and to guide our kids towards safety online.

Here is a good rule of thumb. Social media is intended to create community online, yet virtual friendships are not healthy when they are the core of someone's community. Therefore, I believe that social media should be used as a tool for three main things: enhance personal growth, deepen friendships, and offer healthy entertainment. It is my opinion that if a social media site does not do that, it is not worth using.

Twitter, if used correctly, is a great outlet for personal growth. I personally follow people that I admire and that I believe will add value to me by the things they say and the links they post. Some of these individuals are people I know personally, while others are well-known celebrities, authors, and bloggers. Others represent organizations and companies that I like. All of them help me gain a bigger perspective of myself and the world around me.

Facebook and Instagram are good examples of sites that help deepen friendships. I follow actual, personal friends on these sites, and I feel like it draws me closer to them than I would otherwise be able to get. Some of these friends live in other parts of the country or the world; and therefore, without these social networks, I would never be able to keep up with them at that level.

Even though for teenagers, many of their Facebook friends and Instagram followers are people they see at school every day, the interaction they share by posting pictures and comments adds to the community they already have.

Youtube is a very entertaining site. We have all become a very visually entertained society, and watching videos is part of that. Obviously, with a public video site, there is the chance that some of the videos will not provide "healthy" entertainment, but of the millions online, there are plenty of decent videos on Youtube that are funny and entertaining.

In my opinion, there is a big question mark that comes with the other social media platforms mentioned in this book and the potential value they may or may not create. Can Kik Messenger be used for developing personal growth, deepening friendships, or providing healthy entertainment? Possibly, especially if it is used honestly and not as a secret texting source for younger teens. But what about Snapchat? How does that site rank against those three criteria? I think it depends greatly on the user. Obviously, Snapchat is not going to be used for personal growth, but it could add some value to friendship, and also provides entertainment. With that being said, using Snapchat may be like lighting a candle in that dynamite store for some kids. There is something very mischievous about a picture and text that disappears within ten seconds, never to be proven or seen again.

Tumblr, Ask.fm, Yik Yak, and Whisper are all too hardcore, I believe, for younger teenagers, and even unhealthy for older ones. All of these sites have little to no filter for pornographic pictures or descriptions, and none of them help anyone to add true value to themselves or others, although all three can be highly entertaining, especially to a teenager. My biggest fear with sites like Ask.fm or Whisper is that teenagers might be truly seeking help and counsel and fail to find anything worthwhile other than the click of a like button.

One interesting thing to mention is that six out of the ten social networking sites that I have reviewed in this book were created by college students. At the time the software was developed for those six platforms, the creators were in their early twenties, and still in or just finishing college. As amazing as that might seem, it's no wonder that both of these sites are designed perfectly for the mind of the 21st century teenager, as well as most reckless and potentially dangerous in concept and nature.

Ten Social Media Guidelines for Parents

Below are ten guidelines for parents regarding dealing with teenagers and social media. As I wrap up this book, I strongly advise you to adhere to these suggested guidelines so that you can protect your kids from the dangers and temptations of online networking sites.

Too Young is Too Young - If your child is under the age of 13, he or she is not supposed to be using social media. This minimum age was set up by the Children Online Privacy Protection Act. Some of these sites ask for a birth date, while others do not, but the understood minimum age for all of them is still 13 years old. I understand how hard it is for parents to disallow tweens to have social media profiles when all of their friends are doing it but think of what they are learning. Think about what those other tweens are learning, not just from the content they are seeing, but also from the fact that they have to lie to get an account on these services. If this is a problem, consider talking to the other parents and try to make a collaborative effort to keep pre-teens from pre-mature social media exposure.

Check Privacy Settings - Every Social Media site is going to have privacy features. Some are more secure than others, but be sure you check those, with your child, so that they are set as strictly as possible. These settings will help decide how others can communicate and view content on your teen's proflie. For younger teenagers, I suggest the strictest of settings so that only approved friends/followers can see them online.

Invest In Parent Filtering/Monitoring Services - Every family computer needs Internet filtering software. This is downloadable software that will prevent a computer from going to questionable websites and viewing unauthorized content. The settings can be set for different levels of access and some services can have different settings for different members of the family. One such service is NetNanny (netnanny.com). Also, there are mobile phone monitoring services as well, and, depending on your level of trust, there are a lot of options in this category. These services will allow you to see a call log, text messages, and list of apps that have been opened. Some of these services include mobile phone tracking as well (though there are a lot of apps that will do only this as well). One common monitoring service is My Mobile Watchdog (mymobilewatchdog.com).

Create Online Ground Rules - We have family rules for others things at home, why not have online rules as well? These rules should govern who uses the computer and for how long, what sites are off limits, and what the consequences are if these rules are broken. These rules should also be extended to mobile devices (phones, tablets), because they are now little mini-computers. More examples of these rules might be getting permission before going on a social media site, permission before downloading an app (note: Apple records all app downloads even if they are free, and that information can be found on the account page of iTunes), parents know all passwords, no chat rooms, and no instant messages or texting with people the parents don't know or haven't approved.

Be "Friends" With Your Kids Online - One way to keep your child safe is to be a friend (or follower) of your kids on social media. This way you can see what they post and what comments are made on their Timeline. You might agree to never communicating with them publicly on social media as long as you can friend or follow them.

Be A Good Social Media Example Yourself - Often times the parent becomes a poor example to follow online, as they like and do things that they would never want their kids to do and say. Even though you may feel you have the right, be a good example online.

Teach Your Kids The Importance Of A Good

Online Reputation - You don't have to look hard online to see stories about kids getting thrown out of college for social media posts, or not getting a job because of drunk pictures on the beach in college. An online user's activities are an extension of their integrity and character, and our kids need to understand that those things are not somehow disconnected from online behavior.

Discuss Online Dangers - Kids know that there are bad people out there, and you probably taught them not to talk to strangers. The same rules need to apply to online conversations as well. This is why some of these sites that don't require a following are dangerous; they intentionally invite dangerous individuals to take advantage of unaware kids. Secondly, all teenagers need to remove their personal information (phone number, address, etc.) from their social media accounts. These are publicized and can be accessed easily.

Establish Online Non-Negotiables - A non-negotiable is something that is off the table for consideration. As you set online rules and discuss online dangers, consider helping your child develop a list of things that they commit to never doing online. One example is creating a secret social media account. Sometimes kids will have one social media account that you know about and another that you don't know about that is set to block you from seeing their posts. Another example of a non-negotiable could be to never meet face-to-face with someone they met online. These non-negotiables are intended to protect your child and help them build trust with you.

Become A Social Media Expert - Chances are this book is filled with things that you had no idea about. That is the case for most parents. Many adults know that there are dangers and concerns with online activity, but are not sure what they are or how to handle them. The more you know about the ever-changing world of social networking, the better equipped you will be to lead your children through it. Within one year of this book being written, the list of the most popular social media platforms will have changed, and in a few years, the list will look altogether different. That is the world of today's technology. I suggest that you do an Internet search twice a year for the most popular and newest social media sites for teenagers. If you find something that is not on my list of ten, you might have found one that is new or has risen in popularity.

Conclusion

When I was growing up in the 80's, the biggest cultural distraction for parents was probably MTV. Music Television was the 24-hour video playing obsession for those of us who loved music and videos. I spent many hours watching videos with my finger on the channel changer in case my mom walked in the room, because I knew that I was sometimes watching something inappropriate. In the same way, teenagers today know what these social media outlets are and what they do. Kids talk about it at school and are telling tales about what they have read and seen. Chances are the average teenager has heard about all ten of these social networks that I presented, and most of them are involved with at least a few of them. The question is, what kind of influence do these sites have over them and how will you, the parent, protect them from the biggest cultural distraction of this generation?

The selfie is not going away. It will continue to consume kids and change the way they see themselves. As parents, it is our job to help our children develop a realistic and proper perspective of themselves by allowing them see who they really are, without all of the outside noise that will try so hard to creep into their hearts and minds.

NOTES:

_____

_____

_____

_____

_____

_____

_____

_____

_____

_____

Appendix

Social Media Glossary
Hashtag Index
A Message To Teachers & Youth Workers
About The Author
Notes

SOCIAL MEDIA GLOSSARY

A

App - Short for application, an app is a self-contained software program that performs a specific operation on a computer or mobile device.

Ask.fm - A social media app where users ask questions and receive anonymous answers from other users.

Avatar - An icon or caricature that represents a person's online persona for gaming or an Internet forum.

B

Bitly - An online service that can shorten a website address (URL), usually so that the address will fit into a character-limiting platform, such as Twitter.

Blog - Short for weblog, a blog is a regularly updated web page designed to journal thoughts, content, and picture media.

Blogosphere – A word used to describe the internet-wide community of blogs.

Blogroll – A list of favorite blogs and links found on an individual's blog or website.

Buzzfeed - A popular website that hosts viral content that drives social sharing.

C

Chatroom - A webpage that allows users to communicate with each other, typically about a certain topic.

Channel - A Youtube user's personal page of posted videos.

Check in - A location alert that users can send out on certain community-based social media platforms.

Cloud - an online hard drive of sorts that allows digital files to be stored on internet-based servers for the purpose of sharing, storing, and accessing data remotely.

Circles - An organized group or cluster of users of the social network Google+.

Comments - An expression or idea shared by one internet user in response to an online post by another user, usually on a blog or social media platform.

Connections - The equivalent of a Facebook Friend on the social network Linkedin.

Craigslist - A localized commerce website where individuals sell goods and services in a particular city or area.

Crowdfunding - An internet-based fundraising campaign for a specific cause or effort.

Crowdsourcing - The seeking of input or information by a large number of people online.

D

Delicious - An internet service for bookmarking web content for storing and sharing.

Digg - A news-based website where users submit content and then rate that content by "digging" it.

Direct Message (DM) - A private message between two users on Twitter.

E

Ebay - An e-commerce site where users buy and sell goods globally.

E-book - An electronic version of a book that readers can view on a computer or a handheld reader tablet.

Embed - To copy an internet code of external web content into your own website.

Eventbrite - A website for buying and selling tickets to a live event.

F

Facebook - A popular social media platform allowing users to create profiles, post content, and communicate with friends, classmates, and colleagues.

Flash Mob - A large organized public gathering that appears random but is actually very choreographed.
Flickr - A website for post and sharing photos and videos.

Forums - Also called message boards, an online forum is a website where participants communicate about a certain topic by posting messages.

Follow Friday (#ff) - A weekly activity on Twitter where users recommend someone to follow every Friday by using the hashtag #ff.

Foursquare - A localized social media app that allows users to register their presence at public locations, allowing followers to see where other users are and have been.

Friends - The name for mutual followers on Facebook.

G

Geolocation - The exact geographical location of an individual or object coordinates embedded into a website, picture, or video online.

Google+ - A community-based social media platform, by Google and similar to Facebook, where users form groups and communicate and share content.

Gowalla - A localized social media app, very similar to Foursquare, that allows users to check-in at locations and publicize that location to followers.

GPS - Short for Global Positioning System, a GPS is a satellite-based navigation system that provides you a location and directions on an electronic device.

H

Hashtag - a word or phrase preceded by the pound sign (#)

used to identify a topic in certain social media platforms like Twitter and Facebook.

Hosting - space provided on an internet server for the use of a website.

HTML - Short for Hypertext Markup Language, HTML is the standard system of code for websites on the World Wide Web.

Hyperlink - A link, usually attached to a word on a website that, once clicked, will take the user to a specific online location.

I

Instagram - A popular social media platform for posting and sharing photos and video clips with followers.

Instant Messaging - An online method of communicating through a private chatroom in real-time.

K

Kik Messenger - An Instant Messenger mobile app that allows users to obtain a profile without a phone number and communicate with approved friends through text, photos, and video.
Klout - A web service that uses social media analytics to rank social media users by level of influence.

L

Lifecasting - The process of broadcasting an individual's

daily activities with live video steaming using a portable webcam.

Like - To approve of a post or statement made on Facebook.

Linkedin - A social media platform designed for the business community.

M

Mashup - A hybrid website that combines functionality and data from different websites into one online source.

Meme - A viral text image that is often funny and culturally relevant.

Metadata - A specific set of data providing detailed information about other data.

Microblog - A short-form web log like Twitter where a user makes short posts, as opposed to what might be shared on a traditional blog.

MySpace - A social media platform, much like Facebook, with a strong emphasis on music, bands, and performers.

N

News Feed - A list of updates from your friends on the main page of Facebook.

O

Open Graph - The ability for some social networking platforms to interact with other networks to share information about a user, their interests, and friends/ followers.

P

Pandora - A web service that provides free music streaming.

Permalink - A direct or permanent link to a webpage, often a blog or forum, that will not change, usually including the website host's address rather than the user's domain name.

Pinterest - A social media site where users pin interesting pictures and content to their board to share with others.

Podcast - A digital audio medium where someone records a broadcast and publishes it online for download.

Profile - A page displaying a user's personal information on certain social media outlets.

Protected Tweets - Private tweets by an individual who selected to restrict tweets only to approved followers on Twitter.

Q

Qik - A video messaging service provided by Skype.

R

Reddit - A social media news platform where users can submit and read content.

Retweet (RT) - To re-post a Tweet on Twitter.

RSS Feed - Short for Really Simple Syndication, a RSS feed is used to syndicate online content, like blog posts, to subscribing readers.

RSS Reader - A platform to collect and read content collected from a RSS feed.

S

Scribd - An online, subscription-based digital library of eBooks and audio books.

Search Engine Optimization (SEO) - An online marketing technique to maximize the number of website visits by appearing high on the list of results from an internet search.

Skype - An online communication platform for making worldwide calls and video calls over the Internet.

Short Message Service (SMS) - A traditional text message on a mobile or internet communication system.

Snapchat - A social media platform that allows users to send and receive photo and video, with text that disappear within one to ten seconds after viewing.

Social Media - Websites and applications that allow users to communicate and share content with others participating in the online network.

Social Networking - The process of connecting with others using websites and online applications.

Smartphone - A mobile phone that performs many other functions like internet access, email, and the running of downloadable apps.

Streaming - A method of sending and receiving data online as a continuous flow, as opposed to first downloading or uploading the content.

T

Tablet - A flat mobile computer with touch screen functionality, such as the Apple iPad.

Tag - An organizing category name given to online content for identification and search purposes.

Timeline - The location on Facebook where a user's own shared content is listed.

Thread – A conversation trail on a social networking platform or forum, usually beginning with the original post and including all the comments connected to that post.

Tumblr - A microblogging and social media site that prides itself on creative self-expression.

Twitter - A popular social network that allows users to send and receive 140-character messages called "tweets."

Tweet - A 140-character post on Twitter.

U

User-Generated Content (UGC): A phrase that refers to online material that has been created by the public as opposed to the owner of the website.

V

Vimeo - A popular video sharing website similar to Youtube.

Views - The number of time a certain video has been watched on Youtube or other video-based platforms.

Viral - The process of content circulating quickly on the internet and becoming instantly known or seen by millions.

Vlog - Short for video blog, a vlog is a blog using video instead of text to share content.

W

Web 2.0 - The development of a new purpose for the World Wide Web, taking the internet from standard read-only websites to the user-generated, content sharing world of social media.

Webcast - An online video broadcast of a live event.

Webinar - A seminar broadcasted online.

Wi-Fi - A technology that allows internet-capable devices to surf the web wirelessly.

Widget - An application that goes on a website interface

and enables certain functions.

Wiki - A website that allows collaborative editing of content by users.

Whisper - A social media app that allows users to post confessions anonymously and receive replies from other platform users.

Y

Yik Yak - A social media application that allows users to anonymously post comments, known as Yaks, only to be seen by other users within a 10-mile radius.

Youtube - popular website used for sharing and viewing videos.

HASHTAG INDEX

The following list of hashtags only includes ones that are
unique to teens and may be cause for alarm. A hashtag can
be about anything but there are some, like the ones below,
that are commonly used for specific purposes.

Self-harm, Suicidal, & Depression:

#suicidal
#razors
#harm
#selfharmmm
#selfinjury
#dead
#selfhate
#cuts
#worthless

#broken
#helpme
#useless
#cantsleep
#killme
#secretsociety123
#suicidalquotes
#imnotokay

Self-Image & Eating Disorders:

#thighgap
#thinspiration
#skinny
#thinspo
#bulimic
#anorexic
#depression
#ana
#bulimia
#fakesmile
#eatingdisorder
#bonespo

#hipbones
#purge
#anorexia
#worthless
#anxiety
#mia
#binge
#paranoia
#depressed
#blithe
#collarbones
#blades

Bullying hashtags:
#derp - stupid
#butters - ugly
#jelly - jealous
#subtweet - talking about someone without using their @name
#gokillyourself
#bizzle - another word for b***h
#thot or #thotties - a promiscuous girl
#yag - you are gay
#beyouch - another word for b***h
#rab - rude a** b***h
#frape - Facebook rape (posting to someone's profile when it's left logged-in)

Drug/Sex Hashtags:
#chirped = got caught
#420 = marijuana
#cu46 = See you for sex
#lmirl = let's meet in real life
#pron = Porn
#nsfw = not safe for work (something they shouldn't do while at work)

Popular & Common Hashtags:
#lol - laugh out loud
#selfie - taking a picture of self
#turnt - have fun; get rowdy
#tbh - to be honest
#nah - no
#ff - Follow Friday
#smh – shaking my head
#tbt - Throwback Tuesday/Thursday
#igers - Instagrammers

#igaddict - Instagram addict
#idk- I don't know
#yolo - you only live once
#idek - I don't even know
#bae - babe
#mcm - man crush Monday
#wcw - woman crush Wednesday
#SundayFunday - Relax on Sunday, Fun day
#hmu - hit me up
#so - Significant Other
#lmao - laughing my a** off
#ootd - outfit of the day
#ratchet - disgusting
#sick - cool
#wtf - what the f***
#NoSleep - tired after a long day
#bringitback - asking for an old style/fashion to come back
#Hashtag - when you have nothing else to hashtag
#ThisShouldveBeenAText - too personal to have been shared publicly
#instagood - a really good picture on Instagram
#photooftheday - a good picture posted on social media
#love - one of most popular hashtags.
#me - usually follows a selfie.
#follow - often comes after a link or a #ff
#tagforlikes - often gets noticed, then liked since you asked
#foodie - because so many people post pics of food

A MESSAGE TO TEACHERS & YOUTH WORKERS

If you lead teenagers in a school, church, or community-organizational capacity, it is my hope that this book will help you to educate yourself and the parents represented on the topic of social media. If you would like to teach this material to parents, I have a free downloadable teaching guide for you to use online if that would be helpful to you. The only thing that I ask is that every parent in your seminar has a copy of the book to take home and review. The teaching guide can be found at www.thetransmission.org/resources as well as a special book bulk rate at www.thetransmission.org/store. If you would like for me to come and teach the seminar, please email me at tommy@thetransmission.org.

ABOUT THE AUTHOR

Tommy McGregor is an author, speaker, and the founder of TheTransMission, an organization devoted to helping prepare high school seniors for the challenges of life in college. He is the author of Lost in Transition: Becoming Spiritually Prepared for College, The Freedom Permit: Creating A Vision of Discipleship for your Senior's Last Year of High School, as well as numerous published articles, e-books, and leader training resources. Tommy has spent over two decades working with high school and college students, and speaks regularly to teens, parents, and youth leaders. He lives in Montgomery, AL with his wife Andrea and their two boys, Webb and Wolf.

Tommy can be contacted directly via email at tommy@thetransmission.org, as well as on Twitter at @tommymcgregor.

NOTES

[1] Source: CNN dot com 11/19/13

[2] Source: The Tonight Show with Jimmy Fallon 12/16/14

[3] A children's nursery rhyme that first appeared in *The Christian Recorder* in March of 1862

[4] Source: New York Times

[5] Source: ContentWatch

[6] Source: Nobullying dot com

[7] Source: netnanny dot com

[8] Source: The Atlantic dot com

[9] Source: Business Insider

[10] Source: digitaltrends dot com

[11] Source: tumblr dot com

[12] Source: Whisper dot sh

[13] Source: Whisper dot sh

[14] Source: Wikipedia

16651179R00056

Printed in Great Britain
by Amazon